Decisions Determine Destiny:

Stories & Scenarios

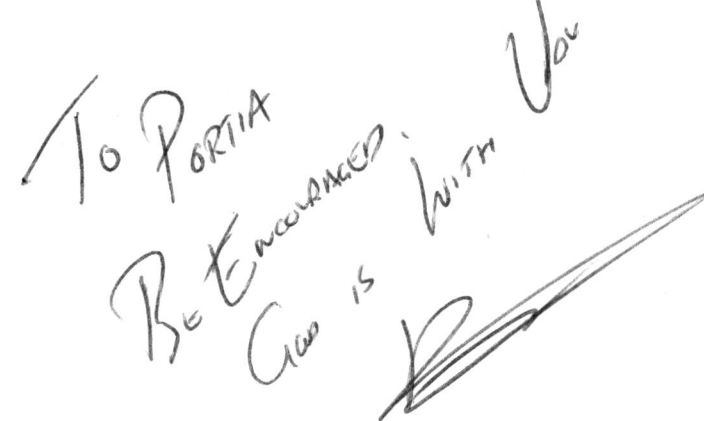

To Portia
Be Encouraged.
God is with You

Kevin A Treasure

Cover design by Absolute Covers
Book design by Absolute Covers
Kevin Treasure

Visit my website at www.decisionsdeterminedestiny.com
Printed in the United Kingdom

Ordering Information:
Quantity sales, Special discounts are available on quantity purchases by corporations, associations, schools and other organisations. For details, contact the author at:
www.decisionsdeterminedestiny.com

Orders by U.K. trade bookstores and wholesalers.
Please contact Decisions Determine Destiny Productions Ltd:
Tel: 0844 504 2396
Mob: (0)7903 940 399
Email:kevintreasure@decisionsdeterminedestiny.com

Special Note of Appreciation

I would like to thank my darling wife, Michelle Treasure, you're a constant source of encouragement, I love you babe. My mother, Mary Treasure thank you for all you've done, without you I wouldn't be here. Janet and Cartlon Morgan you and your family are a constant inspiration to me. All the young people at GIMM continue to stay strong and be positive. Roger Williams thank you for your time and input, keep up the good work. Bonny Paul many thanks, Paul Rose (Start Today), Paulette Thomas thank you for your input, Merlene Huie, (It's amazing where a small conversation on a staircase can lead.) Sherma Walcott-Xavier, your expertise was priceless.

And all my friends and family who believed it could be done, it means so much and more.

A Very Special Thanks

Contents

Introduction

Decisions Determine Destiny is a series of plays designed to bring stories to life through acting and play, allowing the students to become immersed in roles which any young person could find themselves in. Re-enacting the lives of characters in the stories and discovering how people can arrive at certain decisions which can sometimes be a catalyst of positive change or negative consequences.

The Decisions Determine Destiny series (DDD) is a book of plays, which are intended to be part of the Life Skills series for young People. DDD has been specially designed for P.S.H.E classes but can also be used for; G.C.S.E. Drama, Pupil Referral Units, Mentoring Units, youth groups and drama workshops.

DDD encourages teenagers to make the right choices when faced with real issues which sometimes arise in life. Experimenting through role play the many different circumstances they can find themselves in and ways in which they can deal with those circumstances if and when they arise. Using drama as a way to introduce life skills training for young people DDD gives the young people the opportunity to write, practice and perform the stories and scenarios proposed in the book.

The plays are designed to show ways in which a right decision can have a positive impact on their life and the lives of those around them and the consequences of the wrong decisions they may chose and the tragedy which can often follow.

The plays are all group orientated and are always performed in groups. In group work the aim is to give the young people the freedom to experiment with the story, sometimes they will have a chance to take a scene from the story and re-create it, re-enact the story, create alternative endings and script and perform extra scenes . This will always be done by using various modes of drama techniques i.e. Thought-tracking, Narrating, Hot-seating, Role Play and Marking the Moment. Most of the plays are 5-10 minutes in length and will always involve the young people working in groups.

TARGET AUDIENCE: Schools, Youth Groups, Drama Workshops, G.C.S.E, Drama Departments and Mentoring Units.

ISSUES DEALT WITH:

Relationships/Love/Sex/Health/Career/Job/Unemployment.

Achievement/Failure/ Friendships/Peer Pressure/Goals.

THE GROUP WORK:

The group work will usually consist of script writing, drama, prepared improvisation and producing scenarios to complement the stories, giving the young people the opportunity to explore different ways of presenting the drama. Working in this way gives the class the ability to enhance creativity, communication, write and script their scenes, look at character development, and narrative structure. The group work is arranged to take place before the discussions, as often you may find that as the young people take part in the practical work, and act out the given roles (experiencing and feeling the attitude of the character they are portraying) will sometimes provoke them to discussion.

(The group work is optional depending on group sizes.)

THE DISCUSSION:

The discussion time will give the young people the opportunity to express their views on the topics raised in the stories and their group work. The questions are usually open-ended designed at provoking debate amongst the young people. The questions are all based on the text/play they have studied. The discussions will also give an insight to how other people may feel in the roles they adopted and what they would do when faced with challenging issues. The discussions should always try to identify the turning point in the characters life

ISSUES FOR DISCUSSION.

What was the main problem in the story?

What was the turning point in the main characters life?

Were there any issues that helped them make this decision?

Was the decision they made negative or positive?

Could the outcome have been avoided?

What decision would you have made, being placed in the same position?

Do you know any similar stories? What was the outcome and how was it dealt with?

Note for Teachers

As part of the 'Decisions Determine Destiny series, teachers are encouraged to allow the young people involved to consider and act out alternative endings for the stories they chose to play, giving the young people more freedom to experiment with the story and allowing them to play a role in directing and creating their own stories.

Some of the stories contained in these series of plays contain real issues which some of your young people may be going through (or have gone through) in their life. Some may want to discuss with the teacher or youth worker privately and some may be willing to share with the class openly in the discussion, depending upon the sensitivity of the person/issue. As the teacher/ youth worker it would be up to you how to best tackle the issues raised.

Personal, Social and Health Education (PSHE)

Decisions Determine Destiny has been specially formulated for PSHE classes, as the stories and discussions are prepared as part of the life skills teaching for young people. The plays and discussions in the book have been selected to help cover the curriculum needed for PSHE.

Below I have listed the plays in the book which complement the curriculum for P.S.H.E.

THE CURRICULUM	THE PLAYS
Drugs and Alcohol Education:	Love/Lust, Higher Learning, Past Catching Up
Emotional Health & Well Being:	Deep Depression, Noise Nuisance
Sex & Relationship Education:	Love/Lust, Happily Married, Motherly Love, Parents R Not Us

Nutrition & Physical Activity:	Deep Depression, Football Crazy
Personal Finance:	Opportunity Knocks, Job Hunt, Higher Learning, Past Catching Up
Careers Education:	Higher Learning, Job Hunt
Work related Learning:	Job Hunt, Opportunity Knocks

You may find that some children may not chose to take part in the practical part of the lesson. Some children may be too shy to act so teachers may chose to focus more on the discussion. The stories are short enough to read through together and can still be discussed in groups.

Note for Teachers;

Again it is good to stress that some of the discussion points maybe sensitive areas to some pupils. If students do not feel comfortable discussing the issues it would be the teacher's discretion to decide the best way to handle the subject area. Once again the discussions should always identify the turning points and the decisions they made that resulted in their outcome and discuss if it could have been avoided.

Mentoring

Decisions Determine Destiny can be used by mentors in their mentoring sessions. Mentoring is the long term passing on of support, guidance and advice to the mentee. A mentor is usually a guide who offers help to a younger person to find the right direction and who can help them to develop solutions to career issues. Mentoring can be an effective, personal development and empowerment tool for the person being mentored.

Mentoring can also be used as a form of long term development of the character and personality of the person being mentored.

When used in a mentorship program DDD can bring to light the power of right and wrong choices and the effects that follow. In mentoring, it is usually understood that the mentor uses his or her own experiences to help the young person being mentored make better choices. DDD allows the mentor to use various stories that both the mentor and young person can identify with and use the stories to discuss the impact of the choices made in the plays. The stories can be discussed in group format or in a one to one setting.

Benefits of Using Decisions Determine Destiny for Mentoring:

> Help build the relationship between mentor and person being mentored.

> As the meetings between mentor and mentee are usually informal the stories and discussion time can be shared in a more relaxed setting.

> The stories used are both relevant and topical so that mentor and mentee can both relate to them.

> The stories can provide guidance for the person being mentored to prepare them for circumstances, issues and problems that may arise in their future or maybe happening in their life now.

> The stories and scenarios when discussed can bring about an increased self awareness of the choices young people make which helps in building a stronger character.

> Helps encourage young people and challenges them to seek progress regarding their education, career and relationships.

> The stories and scenarios will allow the mentee to explore new ideas and concepts.

- Gives the young person a chance to look more closely at their self, their own issues, opportunities and what they want in life.

- Opens up discussion points for topic areas not usually brought up.

Many mentors have found the stories and discussions more valuable in the mentoring sessions as the group work usually needs four to five people to make it effective. However, the group work is optional.

Pupil Referral Units

Decisions Determine Destiny has been popular within Pupil Referral Units. Pupil Referral Units (PRUs) are a type of school, sometimes within a school set up to provide education for children who cannot attend mainstream school.

They cater for a wide range of pupils, those who cannot attend school because of medical problems, teenage mothers and pregnant schoolgirls, pupils who have been assessed as being school phobic, and pupils awaiting a school place. They also provide education for pupils who have been excluded from school. For most pupils and teachers, the main focus of PRUs should be on getting pupils back into mainstream school.

In today's society, every child is entitled to an education; there are some children who cannot be educated within the confines of an ordinary school environment. So the Pupil Referral Units exist to allow those children who cannot attend school for a variety of reasons to have a chance to gain the same standard and levels of education as those children who attend mainstream school.

Some pupils have entered into the Pupil Referral Unit due to the choices and decisions they have made. DDD will give the pupils the chance to observe within the stories how wrong choices and decisions, affected the lives of the characters in the plays, and can highlight how their own choices can greatly affect their own lives. Using the discussion time adequately can help the young people in coming to terms with some choices they may have made and help them in beginning to make the right choices.

Benefits of Decisions Determine Destiny for the Pupil Referral Unit:

> The stories and scenarios will allow the pupils to explore new ideas and concepts that they may not have considered.

> Provokes discussion and debate among the pupils.

> Gives the young people a chance to voice their opinions.

> Encourages group work and group participation.

> Stories and Scenarios gives the young person a chance to look more closely at their own lives, their own issues, and inspire them to aggressively seek after their own goals in life.

> Helps encourage young people and challenges them to seek progress regarding their education, career and relationships.

> The discussion segment has encouraged many young people to open up during discussion time.

> Allows young people to be more meticulous in their thought process.

The Group Work

The group work gives the class the opportunity to work with two or more of the following;

1) In Pairs   2) In groups

Decisions Determine Destiny is a collection of plays containing different circumstances that sometimes arrive in life in our families, relationships, careers and everyday life. The plays included in Decisions Determine Destiny are designed for young people to act out various scenarios

Decisions Determine Destiny will help:

> ➤ Enhance life skills.

> ➤ Teach young people to value the importance of their decisions.

> ➤ The importance of right relationships.

> ➤ The danger of wrong influences.

> ➤ Deter young people from making the wrong choices in life.

After acting out the plays the young people are given the opportunity to:

- ➤ Change the outcome of the story.

- ➤ Introduce new characters.

- ➤ Get an insight into the characters.

- ➤ Discuss the key points and elements to the story.

- ➤ Every story will provoke discussion and debate.

Many of the stories will incorporate one or several of the following drama techniques to be included in the group sessions: (The group work is optional, many young people have fun acting out and discussing the plays.)

Drama Techniques

Drama Techniques allows the children to experiment with the plays and some times allows the young people to delve deeper into the lives of the characters in the play. (The use of the drama techniques are also optional depending upon the group.)

Hot Seating

Were a character is questioned by the group about his or her background, behaviour and motivation. The method may be used for developing a role in the drama lesson or rehearsals, or analysing a play post-performance. Even done without preparation, it is an excellent way of stepping into a character. Characters may be hot-seated individually. The technique is additionally useful for developing questioning skills with the rest of the group.

Thought Tracking

Thought tracking is the technique of were the inner thoughts of a character are revealed either by the person adopting that role or by the others in the group. Individuals in a group freeze in position and speak their thoughts or feelings aloud. A further development of this is to have the participants draw the distinction between what a character says, what they think and what they feel.

Forum Theatre

This is a scene which is performed twice. Any member of the audience can take the place of one of the characters, enabling a new outcome. During the replay, any member of the audience is allowed to shout 'Stop!' step forward and take the place of one of the characters, showing how they could change the situation to enable a different outcome. Different audience members may explore several alternatives. The other actors remain in character, improvising their responses.

Flashbacks / Flash forwards

Performers improvise scenes, which take place seconds, minutes, days or years before or after a dramatic moment.

Marking the moment

This is a dramatic effect used to highlight a key moment in a scene or improvisation. This can be done in a number of different ways: for example through slow motion, a freeze-frame, narration, thought-tracking or music. It has a similar effect to using a spotlight to focus attention on one area of the stage at a particular moment during a performance.

Role-play

Role play is the basis of all dramatic activity. It is the ability to suspend disbelief by stepping into another character's shoes. Through the structure of the drama lesson this can be used to great effect, challenging children to develop a more sensitive understanding of a variety of viewpoints whilst sharpening their language and movement skills. By adopting a role, children can step into the past or future and travel to any location, dealing with issues on moral and intellectual levels. Thus role-play can be easily utilised to illuminate the themes in the plays.

There's just no helping some people.

Job Hunt

An Original Screenplay

By Kevin Treasure

A young man lies in bed.

NARRATOR

Let's take a look at this guy … he has been out of work a long time and has grown weary. I agree that it can be frustrating when you have been actively looking for work, a high level of rejections can be a real strain on your confidence. This is not the case with this gentleman.

Jerry sits up in bed and lights a cigarette.

(cont..)NARRATOR

He enjoys being on income support. He enjoys sleeping in until 1 o'clock in the afternoon and then hanging out with his friends until 3 am drinking and smoking and then repeating the cycle. He enjoys smoking weed all day and borrowing money off anybody who will lend it to him. He also has a habit of hanging outside schools and dating girls much younger than him. His mother is always arguing with him and his dad has given up. He has no aspirations and no ambition.

Jerry sits up in bed, looks around and then lies back in bed. Downstairs his brother and his mother discuss his future.

NARRATOR

His brother has tried hard to secure him a job.

MUM

Don't do anything for him, he'll only mess it up.

MARCUS

You can't give up on him mum. I found him a job with a friend, it's a great opportunity. After two years of training, he'll be a fully qualified plumber. I know this guy, his company has a good reputation, and he only allows two placements a year. This is good job. Plumbers make good money. If he sticks with it, he'll be making more money than me at the end of it.

MUM

I still feel you're wasting your time.

MARCUS

Mum, give him a chance. I know he can do this.

Mum exits the kitchen, and his brother climbs out of bed and makes his way downstairs.

MUM

You finally decided to get up.

Jerry groans as he sits down and flicks on the television. His brother explains the job and its prospects and manages to convince him he can do it.

NARRATOR

Eventually his brother manages to secure him a place as a trainee plumber, working for four days and studying for one. His older brother is over the moon.

BOSS

The only reason why I am doing this is because he is your brother. People are queuing up for this position.

MARCUS

I am so grateful. I'll make sure he doesn't mess up.

BOSS

He better not. My time is too precious for time wasters. I told you before I've got people queuing up for this position

MARCUS

You've told me that twice. Don't worry.

NARRATOR

His little brother starts his job. The boss shows the young man how to use some tools. While not enthusiastic, Jerry pays little attention during the induction. He also makes him aware of the type of salary he would get if he finishes the course.

(continued) NARRATOR

The first week looked promising. However, on the second week the cracks begin to appear. He's late every day, and some days he doesn't even turn up.

Jerry sits on a couch with a young girl. His phone rings. Jerry glances at his phone. It's his boss. Jerry listens to the first message, he convinces his partner to pick up the phone and tell his boss he can't come in.

BOSS

Hello Jerry, Are you coming in today? It's almost 11.15. If you are not coming in you should always call in to let us know.

He hands the phone to the girl beside him.

GIRL

(Giggling)

Jerry's not coming in today.

Jerry

(Whispering)

Tell them I've got a cold.

GIRL

(Giggling) He's got the flu.

His boss puts the phone down in disgust. Jerry laughs and lights a cigarette for the girl.

NARRATOR

Eventually Jerry loses the job, but in all honesty, he doesn't really care. He never actually wanted the job. His brother is furious.

His older brother Marcus, who is extremely angry, phones him up. Jerry lets the phone ring.

JERRY

(LOOKING AT HIS PHONE) It's my brother. I'm not answering it. I know what he is going to say.

His brother leaves a message on his phone.

MARCUS

How can you do this? How can you be so dumb? You've messed it up for me and for everyone else I could have helped.

NARRATOR

However, Mr. Singh, a fellow worker, manages to get his son a job with the same company in the same position, which has now become vacant.

Mr. Singh and his son enter the boss's office.

BOSS

The last guy messed up. He was a waste of space. If you mess up I'll just close the position. I can't be bothered with the hassle.

MR SINGH

My son is a good boy; he will not let you down.

BOSS

I've heard that before. I don't want anyone wasting my time. I've got a right mind to close the position altogether.

MR SINGH

Just give my son a try. He is a straight 'A' student and this is what he wants to do.

Mr. Singh's son shakes hands with his new boss, and then hugs his dad. They all exit. The boss starts showing Mr. Singh's son what to do.

NARRATOR

Mr. Singh's son not only works hard he excels in his studies and finishes the two years, which flew by. He graduates to become a fully qualified plumber. In fact he excels so quickly that he and his father decide to start their own plumbing business.

NARRATOR

However, Jerry is still hanging out with girls much younger than himself, claiming unemployment benefit, hanging around his estate and causing problems for the local residents. His friends have also given him the nick name "Asbo."

The choices we make determine our destiny. Leaving a training program which could of lead to a lucrative job in the plumbing trade to hang around the estate, smoking and drinking and causing a headache to the local residents is not a wise move. He'll more than likely still be doing the same thing in the next 3 years.

GROUP WORK

In groups get together and devise and write the next scene, which could take place in the main characters life. It could be negative or positive outcome. He could exhibit regret for letting the job go, he could become bitter or uncaring, he may have even come to the realisation of what he had, and he may not even care.

In your groups you will need to write the next scene and act it out. Each group member is to be given speaking parts. You also have the option of introducing new characters. When this is done each group can act out their play as a final performance piece. This can run over two or three classes.

Drama Techniques to experiment with: Hot-seating and Forum Theatre.

DISCUSSION TIME

Do you think the main character realized the opportunity he had?

What do you think was our main characters problem?

1. Laziness

2. Lack of common sense

3. Not realizing the potential of the chosen career

Was the decision of our main character negative or positive?

Could the outcome been avoided?

How did Jerry's actions reflect on his big brother as a person?

Do you feel that some young people need help with the transition from school to work?

As a friend what would your advice have been to Jerry regarding the job he had?

If he did not like the job would he have been wise to either:

1. Continue the job until something else comes up

2. Politely hand in his notice and look for something else

3. Not take it in the first place

How important is it to you when representing other people, (e.g. your school, parents, organization) to make a good impression?

If you had a successful business would you hire someone like Jerry?

(If not, why not?)

Your friends or your future.

Football Crazy

An Original Scenario

By Kevin Treasure

NARRATOR

This young man was encouraged by his mum and dad to pursue his football career. His parents supported him from a young age. At first it was a hobby, something he did on Saturdays, but his parents noticed that he had a real flare for the game.

MUM

If this is what you want to do we'll be right behind you.

NARRATOR

They took him to football every Saturday and Wednesday. They sacrificed their time to always be there. They made sure he always had what he needed for the sport he admired so much. When he wasn't playing it, he was watching it, when he wasn't watching it, he was playing it on his computer. As he grew up he excelled more and more.

ew Arsenal kit is out son, I suppose you want that too?

FOOTBALLER

I need new boots too dad.

DAD

You're growing too fast.

NARRATOR

As he grew he began to excel in his skill and talent for the game. He is eventually scouted for a big name team.

The footballer speaks with talent scout on the field and his parents and friends watch close by. Our footballer and the scout shake hands.

(continued) NARRATOR

As time goes by, his friends begin to start drinking and smoking, getting into fights, some of his friends are even going to jail.

The footballer's friend's start getting into all kinds of trouble some start drinking, some are smoking marijuana, dealing drugs, getting into fights, robbing people and getting arrested.

NARRATOR

Our young friend loves his friends, but finds himself being torn by what he has always dreamed about and his relationship and loyalty to his friends. But it starts to become obvious that his friends are drifting rapidly down the wrong path.

Tony, one of the footballer's friends, drives up next to the kerb in a blacked out BMW and starts talking to him.

TONY

You heard what happened? They stabbed Jerry yesterday. He's in hospital, in Intensive care. It was the man from the estate. We're gonna deal with it properly. You coming?

Tony lifts up his top to reveal the handle of an automatic pistol.

NARRATOR

So many of life's greatest disasters can usually be traced back to a single point in time, were the outcome of destinies rested on one single decision. There are people in prison, abusive relationships, dead-end jobs, and other unhealthy situations because of a single decision they made.

The footballer's friend Nigel steps over to join Tony. .

NIGEL

Come let's go bruv Jerry's my boy. You coming?

FOOTBALLER

(Shaking his head)

I'm cool.

TONY

What? You're not coming? Jerry would do it for you.

FOOTBALLER

I'm not coming. I got to go.

Tony, Nigel, and the other friends drive away, leaving our footballer alone.

TONY

I told you that boy was an idiot.

NARRATOR

Our footballer is too focused to get involved in anything that will mess up his chances of playing the game he loves the most. As time goes on, we find some of his friends continue on the same road. Some are in prison and some are even dead.

The two youths who were inviting our footballer to take retribution on their friend were all caught in one way or another. The police caught

Tony with the firearms and Nigel was captured by a group of males from another gang and beaten very severely.

NARRATOR

Our footballer had to make some sacrifices, let go of some friends, to pursue what was in his heart.

Now he's making £45,000 a week, playing for one of the top premiership clubs. He has bought his mum and dad a house and has ordered them not to work again.

The footballer hands his parents a set of keys to a new Bentley.

NARRATOR

He also does an enormous amount of community work with dis-advantaged kids who are interested in sports…and still finds time to coach young footballers and encourage them to pursue their dreams.

GROUP WORK

Points To Remember:

He was encouraged by parents

He had a strong desire to fulfill his dreams

His friends decided to take the wrong path

A situation arose were a decision had to be made

He overcomes and fulfills his dream

Create a short sketch using some or all of the points made in the scenario you have just read. The main character does not necessarily need to be a footballer, It could be a male or a female, they could have a love for a particular sport, the arts, education or anything you chose to be the focus for your main character.

You are free to add in your own actions and sequences. Create your own dialogue and you can add in your own names.

Drama Techniques to be used: Marking the moment

Characters needed:

Mum

Dad

Son/Daughter

Friends (Maximum 3)

Narrator (Optional)

DISCUSSION TIME

Now in small groups discuss the following questions:

How important to <u>you</u> is encouragement from your parents concerning any ambitions you may have?

Do you feel young people will succeed far more when they are encouraged by their parents?

What qualities do you find in our footballer and the people around him that contributed to making him a success? Examples, goal orientated, focus, vision, undeterred by outside influence, hard work, positive role models, the right encouragement.

How important are goals to you personally?

How can young people avoid people distracting them from their dreams?

How important is parental support and guidance?

How important is it to stay focused on your dreams?

What would you consider more important your future or the opinions of your friends?

What do you personally learn from this story? What will you take away with you?

"I'll get by with a little help from my friends."

The Beatles.

Deep Depression

An Original Scenario

By Kevin Treasure

Lisa sits in a shabby sitting room in her one bedroom flat.

NARRATOR

Lisa is a young female, 22 years old, who broke up with her long-term boyfriend, after that she dropped out of university. Lisa has been out of work for some time, and her mother does not live in the country. Her father has another family, and she does not see him very often. She has not seen her friends for some time either. Everyone is so busy. She spends most of her time indoors. You see that's how it starts. Depression, that is.

The phone rings, Lisa picks it up.

GRANDMA

Lisa, why haven't you come to see me?

Lisa doesn't answer.

GRANDMA

I'm talking to you. I hope you're not still smoking that funny stuff?

LISA

Please Grandma, not right now.

GRANDMA

I want you to come round. I haven't seen you and I am worried about you. I hope you're not still moping around about the boyfriend. I never did like him.

LISA

Grandma I got to go. I'll phone you.

Lisa replaces the handset, puts on her coat to go and meet a friend who also notices Lisa's countenance and her heavy skunk consumption.

MARY

You shouldn't smoke so much of that stuff?

LISA

Don't tell me what to do? You sound like my grandma.

MARY

I'm just concerned about you, you don't call, and you're always smoking. Listen, I know you and Tony were close but,

LISA

(INTERUPTING) I don't want to talk about Tony, and if you're just gonna lecture me I'm leaving. You're as much fun as a clown on morphine.

Lisa gets up to leave.

MARY

You don't have to be rude, I'm just trying to help.

Lisa walks out and makes her way home. Crashes down on her sofa and listens to her voice messages.

ANSWER MACHINE

Lisa, I haven't seen you in ages. How are you? How you been? I've been so busy since I got this job. I'm always up in Holborn. I will try and come and see you. You can call me anytime, we've got so much to catch up on.

NARRATOR

But she never ever gets round to it. Lisa starts to stay indoors, not coming out. She does not want to see anyone and refuses to pick up her phone.

Lisa sits in her bedroom with the curtains shut. The phone rings. Her friend's leave countless messages on her phone.

ANSWER MACHINE

Lisa, Lisa, Lisa, if you're in pick up the phone? You've been on my mind and I am concerned about you. I want to come and see you.

Lisa's friend Maria shares her concerns with an acquaintance in a bar.

MARIA

I saw Lisa the other day.

MALE

I haven't seen her since she broke up with Tony.

MARIA

I'm concerned about her. She didn't seem herself.

MALE

She was with him for ages. Tony told me she was threatening to kill herself and all sorts of things. Saying she couldn't live without him.

MARIA

I need to go and see her.

NARRATOR

When you're going through a rut and there is no one around, you can slip deeper and deeper into depression without even realising. If Lisa had people around her to encourage her she would have been okay. But she shut herself away. However, when you start acting in ways unacceptable to society, the system finds its own way to deal with the problem.

Lisa has excluded herself for so long she begins to exhibit signs of paranoia and psychosis she also starts hearing voices. The next time we see Lisa, she is talking to herself on the street and looking very untidy. In times past people tried to help her, now people try to avoid her. She is eventually taken to a psychiatric hospital.

NARRATOR

All she needed was a bit of support and encouragement.

As she lay's on the hospital bed with her grandmother by her side, the doctor begins to speak calmly to Lisa.

DR.

It would be a good idea if you came in to the ward voluntarily.

Lisa nods her head hesitantly.

NARRATOR

Now she's even worse than before, and her chances of a full recovery are slipping further and further away.

GROUP WORK

Working together in small groups, re-write and act out an alternative ending for Deep Depression. She could get back with her boyfriend, she could stop taking drugs, she could get worst or she could get better. It could be a positive or negative outcome for Lisa. You can use Forum theatre technique to change the ending of Lisa's story.

DISCUSSION TIME

How do you think Lisa felt?

Could the outcome of Lisa's downfall been avoided?

What could have Lisa's friends done to help her?

Were there any warning signs to Lisa's conditions?

What do you know about depression?

As a friend what would your advice have been to Lisa?

What can people do to support their friends who maybe going through difficult times?

Isn't it dangerous to have a friend with mental illness?

Why are people with mental health problems reluctant to open up?

Should people feel responsible for their friends with mental health problems?

Three major studies followed large numbers of people over several years, and showed that those people who use cannabis have a higher than average risk of developing schizophrenia. If you start smoking it before the age of 15, you are 4 times more likely to develop a psychotic disorder by the time you are 26. Are you aware of the strong links between marijuana and mental health?

Do you think most young people who smoke cannabis care about the possible effects?

What do you feel are the best ways to deal with break up?

Do think that young people should be taught how to deal with the break up of relationships?

What would be a good advert to promote the awareness of the links between mental health and cannabis use among young people?

Young hearts, run free

Never be hung up, hung up like…

"Candi Staton"

Wedding Planners

An Original Scenario

By Kevin Treasure

NARRATOR (V/O)

This is Shira. Shira has been seeing David and has been for over a year. However, David is not the choice partner of Shira's family and they have had to keep their relationship a secret as Shira's family would not approve of it.

INT. BEDROOM. DAY

Shira's brother storms into her bedroom, drags Shira's iPod headphones from her ears, as she lay's on her bed.

BROTHER

What's this about you seeing this white boy?

SHIRA

I'm old enough to make my own decisions about who I see, and who I see is none of your business. He loves me and I love him.

BROTHER (INTIMIDATING)

You better stop seeing this man?

SHIRA

Don't tell me what to do? Get out of my room?

BROTHER

If you keep seeing him I'll tell dad.

SHIRA

You won't dare?

BROTHER

End the relationship, if dad finds out you're a dead woman.

Shira's Brother walks out of Shira's room slamming the door behind him as he leaves the room

EXT. PARK. DAY

SHIRA

I've got to move out before my dad finds out.

DAVID

We can get a place together. I'm working you're working.
We can do this together.

SHIRA

David your living in a dream world, my dad will hunt me down. I know what he's like.

DAVID

I'm sick of this meeting in secret,

Not being able to speak to you when I want.

I can't take all this lying and pretending.

SHIRA

We'll work out something. I've got some money saved, we can rent somewhere.

DAVID

My cousin runs a property agency in Chelmsford

We could move down there. No one knows us there.

SHIRA

That's a big move.

DAVID

Do you love me?

SHIRA

Of course I do. (THEY HUG)

INT. DINNING ROOM. DAY

NARRATOR (V/O)

Unfortunately for Shira, Shira's father has found out about their relationship and he doesn't take it too well.

Shira's mother enters the Dining room from the kitchen and leans against the table. Shira's father looks up from his paper.

MUM

Shira is seeing a white boy.

DAD

(SHOUTING) What? How long has this been going on?

How long have you known about it?

MUM

Her brothers told me yesterday. They said they warned her and she refused to listen. She says she loves him.

DAD

I'll kill her. How could she do this to me?

MUM

Don't tell her I told you.

Shira comes through the front door and enters into the Dining room. Her dad lunges out of the chair smacking Shira about the face and head.

DAD

(SHOUTING.) What's this about you seeing a white boy. I'll kill you. I'll kill you. You see that boy again I'll kill you.

Shira's Brother's rush into the dining room to pull their dad off Shira, as he lays into Shira with a barrage of punches. Shira's father over powers his two sons who are frantically trying to pull him off their sister.

BROTHER 1

Dad stop, Calm down, you're hurting her dad.

DAD

I'll disown you; you hear I'll disown you if you see him again.

SHIRA

I love him (CRYING.)

DAD

Shut up, shut up. I hear any talk about love

You don't know what love is. You're going to marry my cousin's son Omar.

SHIRA

(SCREAMING) No, I won't marry him. I don't even know him.

Dad lunges at Shira again while Shira's brothers desperately try to hold him back.

DAD

You'll do what I say, you hear me?

Not what you want, what I say.

Shira runs out of the dining room crying while her father is left screaming his disgust at Shira's mother and brothers. .

NARRATOR (V/O)

Shira's dad has stopped Shira from seeing David. Shira has had to leave her full time job and David has failed at every attempt to contact her.

INT. KITCHEN. DAY

While Shira's Dad walks into the kitchen the phone rings. He picks up the cordless phone.

DAD

Who is this?

DAVID

I want to speak to Shira.

DAD

Shira does not want to see you. Don't call here again you hear me? If you call here again I will call the police on you.

Shira's Dad slams down the phone.

NARRATTOR (V/O)

All attempts by David to see Shira are blocked by Shiras family.

EXT. GARDEN. DAY:

David walks up the path to Shira's house and rings the doorbell. Shira's older brother opens the door angrily and confronts David on the doorstep.

BROTHER

(MENACINGLY) We told you not to come round here. (Grabbing David by the collar.),

DAVID

I want to see Shira?

BROTHER 2

We told you already she does not want to see you.

Leave her alone and don't come back here. (Pushing him to the ground.)

Shira's two brothers attack David viciously.

NARRATOR

Sometimes life can deal some crazy cards. Shira and David were in love. However, circumstances and people can come between that. Tradition can get in the way of destiny.

INT. DINNING ROOM. DAY

Shira's father and a smartly dressed male sit on the couch as Shira's mother brings in two cups of tea.

DAD

I have been talking to your father for some time.

My daughter is a good girl. I am sure she will like you too.

OMAR

I have seen Shira she is very attractive. I believe she will make a fine wife.

Shira enters the room, as she enters her father's smile turns to a glare as Shira stops at the door.

DAD

Shira this is my cousin's son Omar, the young man I told you about.

He's an assistant bank manager.

Shira looks down at the floor. Her father carries on talking to the young man. While they speak the conversation drowns out to show a despondent Shira as she closes the door and walks up the stairs.

INT. OFFICE. DAY

David sits behind his desk clicking on his mouse. His co-workers hurry past him, but David sits back and puts his head in his hands. Roger draws up a chair next to him.

ROGER

Dave, you can't go on like this. It's been nearly six months now. You got to move on

Dave looks at his work mate then looks back at his screen.

ROGER (CONT'D)

  She's married to someone else now David.
She's moved on and it's time for you to do the same.

DAVD

She was forced to marry that guy.

ROGER

How do you know?

DAVID

I just know. They wouldn't let me speak to her they wouldn't even let me see her, If I just got a chance to speak to her.

ROGER

Listen, David I'm telling you this as a friend.Let it go. It's over.

David gets up and walks out of the office.

FOUR YEARS LATER

INT. DINNING ROOM. DAY

Shira now heavily pregnant struggles to get through the dinning room with her two year old daughter clutching her dress, screaming for her mother. Shira clearly flustered trying to balance dinner while trying not to step on her daughter who grabs at her feet.

NARRATOR

I wish I could tell you this story had a happy ending, but unfortunately Shira married Dr Jekyll.

OMAR

You don't do anything in this house. I work all day and you just laze around the house doing nothing. You're useless. I should have never married you

Omar grabs the plate of food from Shira.

OMAR (CONT'D)

What's this? If I wanted crap I would go and buy it.

SHIRA

It's hard to get anything done looking after Kela.

Omar grabs her by the face.

OMAR

What did I say about talking back to me?

SHIRA

You're hurting me.

OMAR

You make me sick, you can't do anything right. I wanted a boy and now you're pregnant again with another girl. You're useless.

Omar release Shira from his grip and pushes Shira onto the sofa. The knives and forks drop out of her hand as she rolls onto the floor. Omar sits back down to eat his dinner. The baby begins to cry as Shira tries to get up off the floor.

OMAR (CONT'D)

You're so fat you can't even get up and shut that baby up.

Shira walks out the dining room with her daughter still running behind her crying. She stops as she enters the kitchen and breaks down weeping bitterly.

NARRATOR

So many people live their lives with regret. Wondering what life would have been like if they taken a particular job, married the love of their life or followed their dreams. In this story we would never know. Shira and David faced many obstacles.

GROUP WORK

Using the main characters of the story act out a piece to the audience describing their feelings about what is taking place in regards to Shira and David's relationship. This could be based at any point of the story; Using Role Play.

For example: It could be Shira's dad when he found out about the relationship, or Shira's mother just before telling her husband about Shira's relationship, David's feeling's about marrying Shira or Shira not being able to marry David, (these are suggestions). This is to be no longer than 2-3 minutes each.

Characters to use:

SHIRA

 DAVID

SHIRA'S DAD

SHIRA'S MOTHER

SHIRA'S BROTHERS

DISCUSSION TIME

In what instances or circumstances do you feel your parents have the right to interfere in your relationships?

Do you believe there comes a point in any ones relationship were parents should get involved? For example; If there was violence or drugs involved for instance.

What do you feel is the right parent approach regarding wrong relationships their teenagers maybe involved in?

How do you handle the topic of relationship with your parents?

What do you do when your parents do not accept your choice of partner?

What happens when you are forced to do something you do not want to?

What do you do when your parent's choices for your life do not agree with your own choices?

Do you think it is wise to remain in an abusive relationship?

Do you feel you could grow to like someone who your parents have chosen for you?

You may be surprised to find that 50 to 60 percent of all marriages of whom the individuals have chosen themselves end in divorce within the first 2 years. However, only 5 percent of arranged marriages end in divorce. Why do you think this maybe?

Your past won't stop your destiny.

Higher Learning

An original story

By Kevin Treasure

A young boy sits in a flat. His mum is about to leave. Noises from the street, fighting, sirens echo through flat.

NARRATOR

This child has had it hard; he grew up on the worst council estate in his borough. His parents were never there, the other kids in school always teased him because he was poor and that his parents were drug addicts.

Mum walks into the living room while her young son is transfixed on the television. He glances at his mother.

BILLY

Are you going out again mummy? Please don't leave me.

Mum turns to talk to the child.

MUM

Don't open the door to anyone. I will be back soon. There's dinner from yesterday, help yourself but just don't open the front door.

Mum exits.

The child sits there for a moment, the arguing from the balcony begin to drown out the cartoon on the television. He starts crying.

NARRATOR

His dad was an alcoholic and his mum was a crack addict. Worse still everyone knew. Kids would tease him on the way home from school.

The child walks home from school. Two children follow him.

CHILD 1

Your mum's a crack head.

CHILD 2

Your mum's a prostitute.

The child runs home. As the two children give chase they begin to hurl stones at him.

CHILD 2

You can run but you can't hide.

NARRATOR

There was never a day that went by that he didn't experience being bullied by other kids. He tried to keep his head down and get on with his work. However, he did have one thing going for him. He was exceptionally bright.

Billy shows his homework report (which he has gained straight "A's") to his dad, who pays little attention.

DAD

What's this then?

BILLY

Here's my homework report. My teacher says –

DAD

(Interrupting) Show your mother.

MUM

Why should he show me? You lazy sod. You never look at his work.

DAD

Who you calling lazy? What you done all day? Why don't you look at it?

MUM

Don't shout at me.

An argument ensues, with the child looking lost and hurt as noise from the argument grows into a blur.

NARRATOR

The school he attends eventually find out about the abuse taking place in Billy's home. The school decides to call in the social services. His mother and father could not care less if their son stayed or left.

A social worker visits the home address, accompanied by two police officers. As they knock at the door Billy's dad answers the door.

SOCIAL WORKER

We are here to pick up Billy.

DAD (SHOUTS)

Billy, get your stuff, it's the old bill.

BILLY

I don't want to go, please don't let me go.

Mum is too high to respond.

SOCIAL WORKER

You're going to come with us Billy

BILLY

I don't want to. Let me go. (As he tries to fight them off kicking and screaming.)

Billy is escorted from his parental home sobbing as his mother and father begins to blame each other for what has happened.

NARRATOR

The child grows up going from foster care to foster care, but he settles with one particular foster parent who spots his unusual gifting in the area of academics.

As Billy sits with foster parent weekly doing his homework, His foster mother begins to nurture his talent for reading and writing and under her guidance begins to excel at an alarming rate.

NARRATOR

With the encouragement of his foster parent, Billy goes on to college to study law and is then accepted into one of the best universities in the country to continue his studies in law. He graduates with a first and honors and is eventually head hunted by one of the best law firms in the country.

He enters into a boardroom. To exchange contracts as they arise they shake hands over the agreed salary.

LAWYER

Welcome aboard. We're happy to have a lawyer with your potential join our firm.

Billy grins as he walks out of the office, where his foster mother is waiting expectantly outside for the outcome. As Billy nods his head his foster mother embraces him with tears of joy for her foster son.

FOSTER MOTHER

I knew you could do, didn't I tell you that you were going to be someone special when you grow up.

BILLY

Thanks for believing in me mum.

FOSTER MOTHER

Your mum is going to be so proud of you.

NARRATOR

Billy has also helped his mum get off drugs. She's cleaned up, has a newfound faith, and has finished her course in counseling. His mother travels the country holding counseling sessions for people who are recovering addicts in the community. Her efforts have been recognized by local government who want to enlarge her scheme to a national level because of the success she has experienced in the area of rehabilitation in the community

While studying Billy helped his mother recover from her addiction, her son's success has motivated her to kick the habit. It's been hard but they have both managed to put the past behind them.

NARRATOR

And Billy, well he has never lost a case, and is often called to speak at his old school to the pupils who are leaving and going on to higher education. Something his headmaster takes pleasure in doing. Against the odds Billy's done well. Against the odds you can make it.

GROUP WORK

In groups take a scene from Billy's life and improvise a piece to the rest of the class. This could be from his childhood how he felt growing up in his home. His school years, the bullying and name calling he receive, his teenage year's (possibly inadequacy about living with a new family.) It could even be his home life or his life as an adult reflecting what he has been through.

It should be no more than 3-5 minutes long. This should be done using 4-5 people.

Drama Techniques to be Used: Thought tracking and Narration can also be used to tell his story.

DISCUSSION TIME

Would you say the foster parent went above and beyond the call of duty for Billy?

What do you believe are the rewards of being a foster parent?

Do you believe your upbringing has a lot to do with the person you will eventually become?

Do you believe your upbringing has a lot to do with what you will accomplish?

What are the benefits of encouragement? Looking at the list below which do you believe is the most significant to you? (1 being the highest, 5 being the lowest)

BENEFITS FOR THE "ENCOURAGEE" (The person being encouraged.)

1. Builds self-confidence and a positive self-image

2. Creates an ally

3. Provides feedback on what they are doing well

4. Provides feedback on how they can do better

BENEFITS TO THE ENCOURAGER (The person encouraging.)

1. Strengthens the relationships

2. Builds trust with others.

3. Provides opportunity to "teach" others

4. Creates an ally/friends/associates

5. Strengthens communication skills

What other benefits would you add to this list?

Think of a person in your life who has encouraged you along the way. What kind of a difference have they made in your life? This could be a friend, family member, teacher, etc.

We must be able to come to some sort of amicable agreement?

Noise Nuisance

An Original Scenario

By Kevin Treasure

NARRATOR

John works nights. He has done for some time. He enjoys his job and works hard. However, his neighbour does not work at all He plays music from the moment he wakes up until late in the night and his friends usually party along with him till the early hours of the morning, on a weekday. His noisy neighbour has no regards for anyone.

INT. LIVING ROOM. DAY

A large male covered with tattoos shaking his head to the music as it blares out the 18-inch speakers. As he turns to his friends he throws a can of Stella, which hits his friend in the forehead. The stocky looking biker rubs his head and picks up the can and throws it at another male who found the incident hysterically funny. This hits him in the chin. A scuffle breaks out creating even more noise of banging and laughing. As the laughing and music and banging continue, they hear a banging on the wall. They all stop, look at the wall, rush to the wall and start banging repeatedly on the wall in response to the banging they previously heard. They all laugh and sit down and open more cans.

INT. BEDROOM. DAY NEXTDOOR

John covers his head with the pillows as the noise echoes through his walls.

NARRATOR

John has tried on many occasions to talk with his neighbour in an attempted to come to some sort of compromise, but all attempts have failed, miserably.

INT. DOORWAY. DAY

John knocks on the door as he waits patiently for it to open. The door opens to reveal a mean looking male.

JOHN (politely)

Can you just turn it down a little? I'm on nights tonight and I really need....

The door shuts abruptly in his face before John finishes his sentence. John looks up and sighs. He walks back to his apartment and shuts the door and climbs back into bed. He picks up the phone and begins to dial.

JOHN

Hello, can I have the police please. Hello police. Yes can you come round and speak to my neighbor. It's been going on for some time and he refuses to turn his music down I work nights and I don't know what to do.

OPERATOR

I'm afraid this is not a police matter; you'll have to speak to the council.

NARRATOR

John has been referred to many different agencies but finds no help. Police, council, Citizens Advice, no one seems to care.

JOHN

But the police told me that they don't deal with this...

But I've already tried the council. I've reported this time and time again...yes I'll hold. (ANGRILY) I've spoken to this man twice already, why don't you come and hear for yourself. I'm not the only one complaining about this man.

INT. BEDROOM. DAY

John is trying to sleep while the walls are shaking due to the vibration of the music. Other neighbours are also complaining of the noise. John picks up the phone and begins to dial.

JOHN

Listen I really need help, I don't want to do anything stupid, I am on the verge of a nervous breakdown. Please can someone help me?

INT. OFFICE. NIGHT

John lies on his desk sleeping while the phone rings

SUPERVISOR

This isn't like you john. Are you still having trouble with your neighbour?

JOHN NODS

SUPERVISOR

You can't go on like this John

JOHN

I've tried every avenue. I can't get help anywhere.

SUPERVISOR

Don't get caught sleeping by the big boss, you can't afford to lose your job because of this.

NARRATOR

Even when his children come round for the weekend there is no let up.

INT. BEDROOM. NIGHT

John tries to read a bedtime story to his two sons while a horrendous noise is taking place in the background.

JOHN

Muffin McClay like a barrel of hay. Snizzel vin crum with a very low tum... I'm sorry about this kids, Let's sleep in the other room.

John takes the kids into the living room and covers them under a blanket.

JOHN (CONT'D)

I need to speak to the noise nuisance department please?

RECODRED VOICE MESSAGE

You've reached the voicemail of Shirley Reid,

I am not at my desk at the moment but if you would like to leave your name along with a short message I will endeavour to get back to you. (BLEEP)

NARRATOR

Sometimes there's only so much a man can take.

Every available avenue has been exhausted.

As John gets up and walks to the kitchen he opens the cupboard to get a glass. As he opens the cupboard door the vibrations from the music cause the cupboard to vibrate, causing all the glasses to fall off the shelf. John pauses for moment, he storms over to his broom closet and pulls out a baseball bat, marches over to his neighbour's door. John rings the bell and waits, as the door opens; John pushes the stoned Biker out of the way and begins to smash up the music system in the front room. John smashes up everything in sight. He goes particularly crazy on the music system.

JOHN

(SHOUTING) So you wanna play music? Well no more, no more you little...

John totally trashes his neighbour's house while a couple lay on the couch in total shock too drunk to do anything.

NEIGHBOUR

(DIALING THE POLICE) I need the police my neighbour has gone berserk. He's got a baseball bat. Please come quickly.

John takes a swipe at his neighbour while he's on the phone, knocking him to the floor while punching and kicking him repeatedly.

INT/EXT. HALLWAY. NIGHT

John is escorted out of the building by two officers and placed into the back of a police van. John hangs his head down as he slowly begins to evaluate in his mind what has just transpired.

JOHN

I called for your help thousands of times and you never ever came.

OFFICER

Violence is never an option sir.

You should always call the police. Never take the law into your own hands.

John shakes his head.

INT. COURTROOM. DAY

John sits next to his barrister as he listened to the case being mounted against him. His neighbour takes the witness stand with his neck in a collar and several bandages about his head and begins to give his version of events.

NEIGHBOUR

He just went crazy. I've never seen him like this, he just went berserk. I was petrified. I thought he was going to kill me. I've never been rude to him.

As the judge begins to sum up, he states.

JUDGE

Your conduct has been one of a wild man. You have caused thousands of pounds worth of criminal damage to your neighbour's property not to mention the horrendous injuries you have inflicted to your neighbour. In light of the evidence against you I have no other option but to sentence you to six months imprisonment. You cannot take the law into your own hands

HAMMER BANGS

INT. PRISON HALLWAY. DAY

John is escorted through the hallway into a small cell.

The door closes behind him. John walks over to the bed and lies down.

In the background shouting and swearing can be heard in the distance,

The prisoners are talking to one another through a window. A loud banging is accompanied by some very loud screams.

PRISONER 1

Keep the noise down.

PRISONER 2

Get lost

JOHN GIVES A DISTANT LOOK,

NARRATOR

John has lost his job. His ex-partner has now filed for full custody of the children, as she does not want to expose their children to erratic, violent behaviour. John who just wanted a good night sleep was failed by the system.

NARRATOR

He tried every available avenue and got no help

As John lies on the bed he contemplates the different people that have passed the buck.

PHONE OPERATOR 1

You need to speak to the environmental health department.

PHONE OPERATOR 2

You need the noise nuisance department.

PHONE OPERATOR 3

Have you tried the police? You could write to your MP.

GROUP WORK

Using the scenario you have just read create and perform the story. This time, telling the story through the point of view of one of the other characters. This could be John's neighbour, John's Boss, The council, John's children, John's ex -wife, other neighbours who are experiencing the same problem or the Judge.

This piece is to show that there is more than one side to a story. Your play could sympathise or disagree with John's point of view. His neighbour may not care; his boss could feel sorry for him, his children could be upset about the situation.

Your act should incorporate body language, facial expressions and accents.

Drama Techniques To Be Used: Role Play and Marking the moment

DISCUSSION TIME

What could John have done differently?

What would you do if you were faced with a difficult, neighbour/ work colleague?

What ways can you resolve a difficult neighbour?

Is there ever any justification in taking the law into your own hands?

Which of the following steps should be taken when dealing with difficult/impossible people?

1. Try to know the motive behind their actions.

2. Before you give them the cold shoulder, try voicing your concerns.

3. Be direct with them and address the problem head on.

4. Deal with it your own way it's the only way they'll learn

When you are faced with difficult/impossible people do you;

1. Find any excuse to start an argument with them.

2. Recognize that impossible people exist, so totally ignore them and hope they'll go away.

3. Keep cool and do your upmost to guard against anger

4. Avoid letting the impossible person make you into a "clone" of them (their behaviour can affect your behaviour.)

5. Always try to be the opposite of them: a possible person

6. Get some perspective from others

What other areas of society do you feel people have been failed by the system and why?

John's decision put him in prison, looking at the story do you think there was another way this could have been resolved?

Opportunities are everywhere.

Whether we seize them is another matter.

Opportunity Knocks

An Original Scenario

By Kevin Treasure

NARRATOR

Meet the Williams family. This is dad, Mark who has been claiming unemployment benefit and disability allowance for three years. He takes cash in hand jobs as a labourer when he can but refuses to get a proper job because if he was to get a proper job the authorities would find out and stop all his benefits. According to their records he injured his back three years ago and is unable to work. Which of course is untrue?

This is Suzy his long-term partner, they made up their mind a long time ago not to marry, because if they did they would lose a lot of benefits. Suzy has never worked. She found out a long time ago if she did work she would have to pay her full rent and council tax and it's just not worth the hassle. She believes.

This is their son Kenny. Kenny is 22 years old. Dropped out of school at 15 with no G.C.S.E. has a bad habit of starting a course every

September and dropping out by December. Works in a pub part time and has no aspirations to do anything else.

And lastly, this is their daughter Mary. Mary is 18 years old and has a two year old daughter and is pregnant again with her second child. She got pregnant with her first child so she could get housed quickly but it hasn't quite worked out. She does not want to work her mother fell pregnant with her when she was young and she is just repeating the cycle.

Now let's look at Alfons. Alfons came here on invitation from Lublin, Poland. When he arrived he stayed with his brother and his brother's wife in a one bedroom flat. When he arrived in England in 2001 he got a job as a labourer. Not long after he got himself a job in a car wash. Eventually he brought the car wash and ended up buying two more car washes.

NARRATOR

Let's listen to their Points of View

FATHER: I like drinking; I like going to the pub with me mates. My Mrs tells me to stop smoking, I smoke 40 a day but she's a hypocrite because she's always nicking my fags. I often sneak down to the bookies when I got a spare £20 but don't tell the Mrs. I get a bit a building work here and there but I can't work on a Wednesday because I got to sign on. I like a kick about on Saturdays but I don't do it often because the social think I'm an invalid. 'cause I claim incapacity benefit, income support and disability allowance. They think I can't walk properly so I always put my crutch in the car and whip it out when I go down the Social.

MOTHER: My other half is a lazy old sod. He never does anything around the house. Gets all this money from the social and doesn't give me any. I lived on the estate all my life; it's changed a lot round here. A lot of immigrants have come over. This estate aint what it used to be. I remember when you could leave your doors open not no more. If you ever need anything from Marks just let me know. I can get stuff cheap from there. My sister works there and she gets stuff for little or nothing.

KENNY: My mum and dad get on my nerves. Always telling me to get a proper job, talk about the kettle calling the pot black. At least I got a job. They get on my nerves. I like going down to the town centre hanging about outside the kebab shop and messing about with my friends. I sell a bit of grass when I can but we always get plastered on Fridays because it's a pound a drink at the student union. I work in a pub part time and I always give my mates free beer when the landlords not about. It's the best little job I've ever had, I'm not leaving this job.

MARY: I'm 18, I know what you're thinking, she's 18 and she's got a baby and she's pregnant again. I don't really care what you think. In six

99

months time I'm going to have my own place. I didn't mean to get pregnant again we didn't have any condoms. It means that might get me a bigger place though. Gary gets on my nerves. Gary's my boyfriend. Fiona told me he's been cheating on me but he's denying it. I feel like calling the Jeremy Kyle Show and let them find out if it's true. He's always telling me to stop smoking because I'm pregnant. He can get lost. It's all right for him to smoke skunk all day. If he wants me to stop smoking he should stop smoking as well.

DAUGHTERS FRIEND: Yeah, I went to school with Mary. She was dumb back then and she's still dumb now. Gary, that's her partner is two-timing her, everyone knows it, but she always denies it and she sticks up for him. She's an idiot staying with him. He's got other kids for other girls and on top of all that she's pregnant for him again. She's dumb. She's got no ambition and she's just like her mum.

MUMS NEIGHBOUR: she knows everybody's business and she's always ponsing fags off people. She always trying to sell stolen Marks and Spencer's clothes, who shops at Marks and Spencer's?

SON'S FRIEND: Yeah! Kenny's always up for a laugh. When he's working we always get free pints. We just act like we're buying and he gives us free beer. He can't read or write to save his life though, but he's a good bloke.

ALFONS: When I came here I lived in a dingy one bedroom flat. My brother slept in one room with his wife and daughter and I slept on the sofa. I did this for nearly a year until I managed to get a proper job. When I came here I couldn't speak a word of English I learned English from my brother and his wife. When I did get a proper job here working on the building site, it was hard. I didn't mind the work but because I didn't speak English I could see a lot of the workers got frustrated with me. It was horrible. There was only one Russian guy who spoke Polish he helped me a bit, showed me the ropes and what to do. I would be picked up at six in the morning and dropped back off at 7pm, but I enjoyed the work. I sent money back to my wife and family every month and managed to save quite a bit too. When the labouring work dried up my cousin asked me if I wanted to come and work in a Car Wash I was a bit unsure because I thought that I wouldn't make as much money as I did as a labourer. But now I am making three times as much as I was as a labourer. After a year my boss told me he wanted to sell the business to me, so I saw the opportunity and brought the business. Now, it virtually runs itself. I managed to purchase 2 other car washes. I have managed to buy a house over here and I've just purchased a house in Poland for my mother. The business is going quite well and a friend of mine has also asked if I would like to go into business with him also in buying and selling properties in Bulgaria. I've accomplished a lot in a short space of time, but it took hard work, but it's paid off.

BOSS: Alfons is one of the best workers I have ever had. He was always on time and never complained. He was the only person I could leave in charge when I was away. He was the only one I could trust with money. When I had irate customers he would just do what they asked and that would always shut them up. I had had enough of the car washing business and Alfons was the only person who seemed capable of actually continuing the business. When I told him I was selling the company I told him he would need seven grand. I couldn't believe he had it saved up. I sold him the business and it's doing fine. I recently contacted him and he has told me he has purchased two other car washes. He is a true entrepreneur considering he couldn't even speak the language 8 years ago.

Alfons's Brother: I am so proud of my little brother; he was always a quite boy, always thinking. I felt sorry for him when he first came to England, couldn't speak a word of English, but he learnt it so quickly, quicker than me. I can't believe how much money he's saved. When he told me he was going to buy the car wash I laughed at him. Now he owns three car wash companies. How he did it I do not know. Now he doesn't even work he just manages and he's raking it in. He's been in the country about eight years and he owns his own house and has two cars.

NARRATOR

Same country, same opportunities different outcome.

GROUP WORK

Read each profile, in groups of 5-6. Each person is to take one of the characters mentioned and building on what you know about their personality, create a two minute piece to the audience which must reflect the person's character, attitude and personality. You can experiment with accents (if you can.) This will be the individual's life and feelings being read out to the class. This could be done to an audience or to camera.

Remember;

1. Read a loud

2. Get Into Character

Characters needed (chose from the list.)

Mum

Dad

Kenny

Mary

Alfons

Alfons's Brother

Alfons's Boss

DISCUSSION TIME

Why do you feel some people achieve more than others?

What's the difference between Alfons and someone like Mark or Kenny?

How important is self-motivation?

Who do you think was less dis-advantaged, And why?

Why do you think Alfons achieved more than the whole Williams family put together?

How important is it to have goals in life?

What things can people do to avoid an un-productive life?

Do you believe your upbringing has a lot to do with your destiny?

In what ways can people use a negative background to become?

1. A springboard to success
2. A downward spiral to failure

"Crime doesn't pay"

Popular proverb, often ignored.

Past Catching Up With You

An Original Scenario

By Kevin Treasure

NARRATOR

Matt left school in September and he hasn't enrolled to college, he has no plans to go back to school in fact, he has no plans to do anything. He has started experiencing pressure by his mother to either go to college or get a job. His home always seems tense, especially when he's there. He and his mother are always arguing and now he tries to stay out of her way.

Mark comes into his kitchen to find his little brother Matt at the table.

MARK

You need to get a job or go to college bro,

MATT

Don't tell me what to do,

MARK

Who you talking to like that, I will slap you up you talk to me like that

MATT

Yeah, whatever,

Mark lunges at Matt, who dives out of the way,

MATT

I'm telling mum, Why you always starting on me?

MARK

I'm trying to knock some sense into you, you've been hanging with them boys, and if your moving with them I know you're up to no good, if I hear your robbing people, I'm gonna knock you out.

MATT

You're not my dad, you can't tell me nothing.

Mark grabs Matt by his clothes, and draws him to his face.

MARK

I know those boys, their brothers went to my school and all their brothers are in jail because they thought they were bad and thought they could go round robbing people, now their little brothers think it's cool to walk in their footsteps, if they're not careful they are going to end up in the same place as their brothers and I don't want you going the same way.

MATT

Let go of my clothes

Mum comes in

MUM

What's going on here? Why you grabbing up your brother like that? Let

him go

Matt grins as Mark releases his grip.

MARK

I warned you already

Mark walks out

MUM

Why you upset your brother?

MATT

He thinks he's a big man

MUM

He is a big man, He's older than you, and you must respect your elders.

Anyway you been looking for a job? What you going to do?

Your cousin Sonya is doing 3 A-levels

MATT

Mum not now. I gotta go,

MUM(SHOUTING)

You think you're going to live under my roof and lay about all day and do nothing, not in my house,

Matt begins to walk out

MUM

Where you going? Don't walk off from me when I am talking to you

Matt grabs his jacket and walks out the house.

NARRATOR

Matt is a very talented young man, but is easily influenced; His brother has warned him about his friends

But when you don't hear, you will usually feel

Matt hooks up with his two companions who convince him about a job they're are about to carry out.

GREG

There's a big house, on Danville Avenue, They always leave their curtains open. They've got a flat screen in every room and a home cinema system. The dad always comes in late and I think the mum does some sort of shift work. If we hit it today we can take our time and get what we want.

TONY

Are you in?

MATT (MATT NODS)

I'm definitely in, I'm sick of being broke.

Late that night the three friends break into the house, while inside the house they rummage around the upstairs, unaware that a concerned neighbour is observing them.

GRANNY (ON THE PHONE)

Hello, Police, There are some hoodies and I think they have just broken into the house next door. They definitely don't live there. You need to get the police here now. Yeah, it's the house next-door get the police here now.

Inside the house.

MATT

We've got enough stuff now come let's go now?

GREG

No, we haven't tried the upstairs bedroom

As Matt turns to sneak out of the back door, a tall dark male greets him.

OFFICER

Going somewhere?

The officer grabs Matt and marches him off round the front of the house.

GRANNY

That's the one officer, that's him, Where's his friends?

NARRATOR

On that night everyone else got away. Matt alone stood trial for the burglary. Knowing the consequences of telling the police who else was involved, Matt chose to remain silent when questioned about the identities of his accomplices. Matt was charged with burglary and pleaded guilty and served 18 months for his crime.

His friends never contacted him once and never ever came to visit him in prison.

NARRATOR

After serving half his sentence he is released on parole

He is met by his mum who embraces him.

MUM

Are you O.K? Did anyone hurt you?

MATT

Don't be silly mum. I'm fine.

MUM

Are you sure?

MATT

Mum I'm O.K. I just want to get back on my feet,

MARK

You were never on your feet bruv,

MATT

Funny, mum I'm out and I am not planning to go back there. I just want to get a job and keep my head down.

MUM

I don't want you mixing up with those boys again. They haven't said anything to me. They didn't even come to see you in prison. They're not your real friends son. Just promise me you won't get involved with those boys again? Promise me?

MATT

I promise mum.

MARK

I did warn you about those boys, Mum's right they're not your friends. All they care about are themselves. Make sure you stay away from them.

MATT

I will bruv.

MUM

Please, Matt for the love of God, I don't want you getting into trouble again.

NARRATOR

For the next three months Matt searches frantically for a job, but to no avail. In filling out job applications he has to mark the box marked "yes" for the part of form marked 'any previous convictions.' He never hears from them again. As time moves on he begins to get desperate. He cannot get a job, as his criminal record always becomes the employer's main focus.

While coming back from the Job centre Matt bumps into his old acquaintances.

GREG

Matt, long time no see, How you been?

MATT

I been better, How can you ask me how I been? You didn't even come to look for me in prison.

ROGER

How could we come and see you when we were your accomplices. That would be suicide. They monitor who comes to see you in there.

GREGG

Anyway we got a better scam.

MATT

Forget it; I am not going back to prison.

ROGER

You don't have to go back to prison, all we need is a driver, all we just need a lift back from Manchester.

MATT

Not interested.

GREGG

We'll give you a grand just to drive us there and back. Matt you're the only one that can drive. You look older, you won't get stopped.

MATT

No funny stuff? We just need a lift to Manchester and back?

GREGG

No funny stuff, Just a lift and you get the money at the end. I know you need the money.

MATT

When?

GREGG

Saturday

Matt thinks long and hard, then answers;

MATT

I'll be there

On the way back from Manchester Gregg leans over and hands Matt an envelope.

GREGG

This will be the easiest grand you'll ever make.

ROGER

I can't believe we're back in London already. I told you it would be easy.

MATT

What was in that package anyway?

As Matt finishes his sentence blue lights flash in the background as they are pulled over by a police van. Roger and Gregg try to run but are caught. All are apprehended and questioned. The vehicle is searched and the package seized. When the package is opened the police find cocaine with a street value of £250,000.

NARRATOR

Matt was on parole, he is immediately brought back to prison to serve the rest of his sentence, while waiting for a trial date for his second offence. His co-defendants are on bail, enjoying their freedom, for now. Matt is back in prison, his mother s heart-broken and his brother is furious. His choice to ignore his older brother's warnings landed him in jail the first time. His second choice to trust the same friends that landed him in prison the first time gave him the same outcome.

GROUP WORK

For this group work you have two options:

Options 1: In groups, select parts for each of you to assume the role of one of the family members. Using thought tracking were the character speaks out loud about his/her inner thoughts at any moment in the drama.

For example for Matt: What are his thoughts and feelings?

He could be saying to himself "I should have listened to my brother? I can't believe I got caught? Why didn't anybody else get caught? I can't spend my Birthday and Christmas in prison. I miss my mum.

Option 2: Using some or all the points below you can use the same script you have just read or create your own story. This must be done incorporating at least two of the following; 1) Marking the moment, 2) Hot-seating, 3) Narrating.

> Young man in the wrong company

> warned not to get mixed up with bad company

> Brother refused to listen,

> Got involved in burglaries and crime

> Got caught on his first time out

> Spent 18 months on first offence

- Everyone else got off.

- When he got out he vowed to his mother to go straight

- Searched for a job started a few but every time the checks came back they sacked him

- Got really excited about starting with a new firm

- Past the test and was great on the interview

- Over the moon when he got the job

- Four months into the job

- He was let go because of the burglary offence on his CRB

- Met up with an old acquaintance

- He is coerced into doing another criminal act

- He'll get a grand for doing it.

- Seemed like an easy way to make money

- Pulled over by the police.

- The vehicle is searched the package is opened

- Cocaine and heroin found

- All men arrested and

- Remanded in custody and eventually tried

- And is now looking at seven years incarceration

> His past held him back from progressing any further

> He reverted back to crime which still didn't pay

DISCUSSION TIME

Issues for discussion:

A warning for young people whom maybe vulnerable to the influence of negative friends and negative peer pressure, the pressures of the lure of money and acceptance by others. Understanding it takes courage to say no when everyone else is saying yes.

Would you rather be accepted by friends or risk your life on a dumb decision?

Would you agree there is a strong urge for most teenagers to make money, by any means necessary?

In your opinion would you say that the majority of young people involved in crime are?

1. Not aware of the consequences involved

2. Know the consequences but do not care

3. Think they'll never get caught

Do most young people your age think more about their present circumstance or their future?

Do you agree that wrong friendships can take you down the wrong road, no matter how sincere they may seem?

Matt found it hard to say no to his friends because he was going through a tough time, is that ever an excuse from crime?

Have you heard of a CRB (Criminal Records Bureau)?

Matt could not get a Job because his past had entrapped him from what he wanted to do today, do you think that is why most people never leave their criminal lifestyle?

Are you aware of all the dangers implicated with illegal drugs e.g. stealing, addiction, overdose, jail?

In your opinion are your peers more interested in making money illegally or finding a job?

Are you ready for this lifestyle?

Probably not.

Parents R Not Us

Baby Dad

An Original Scenario

By Kevin Treasure

NARRATOR

Relationships break up, it's a fact of life. However, it gets a bit complicated when there are children involved. Most parents try to do what's best for the children. However when you are young yourself, you don't necessarily know best for the child, in all honesty you do not know what's best for yourself either. In fact, most teenagers are just coming out of childhood and are not ready for parenthood. Take this guy for example. He got his girlfriend when he was sixteen years old, they did not use any contraception. Surprisingly, they broke up not long after the child was born. His son is now two years old. He has his son on most weekends and whenever he can be bothered.

EXT.PARK.DAY

Gary waits by a park bench anxiously pacing up and down glancing at his watch. A female approaches him hurriedly pulling a young child behind her.

GARY

I been waiting ages.

CHARLOTTE

Makes up for the times you've had me waiting, not to mention the days when you didn't even show up.

GARY

Don't shout in front of him.

CHARLOTTE

You're a fine one to talk, it's all right to shout and swear when it suits you. I aint got time for this. Make sure you bring him back early on Sunday please because I want to go to my mum's and he needs nappies and the jacket you brought for him is already too small.

(As she turns to the child) Mummy will see you on Sunday, O.K. babe.

Mum bends down to kiss her son, as she arises she gives Gary a dirty look before walking off.

INT. HOUSE. DAY

NARRATOR

Gary hasn't spent five minutes with his son before he gives him to his mum and is off to his room with his friends.

Mum at the foot of the stairs.

MUM

Gary, get down stairs now.

GARY

What is it mum? Why are you shouting?

Gary comes downstairs picks up a couple packets of crisp and a few can drinks while his child sit in the living room watching cartoons.

MUM

You can't take the child for weekends and leave him with me all the time. You've got to spend time with him.

GARY

But mum I got my friends round.

MUM

That's not my problem, he's your son and you need to do things with him. Take him swimming or to the library, do something with him.

GARY

But your his grandma, he came to see you as well.

MUM

I know he did, but I spend more time with him than you and it's got to stop Gary, before you know it he'll be in school and running around and you'll find you haven't spent any time with him.

Gary glances over to his son.

GARY

Do you wanna come upstairs with daddy?

Child nods, they both march upstairs into his dads bedroom were a group of teenagers are smoking and drinking and smoking while playing a violent play station game. His son climbs onto the bed and sits there while they carry on talking.

FRIEND 1

Did you sleep with the girl you met in Bromley?

FRIEND 2

Of course I did, you should see her sister?

FRIEND 1

Is she fit?

FRIEND 2

Of course she is, but she wouldn't look twice at you. Not with a nose like that. (LAUGHING)

GARY

Shut up and pass the rizla.

As they continue to talk as if there was no child amongst them, they continue to drink and smoke and fill the air with smoke, while his son begins to play with some toys he found on the bed.

GARY

(TAKES FIVE SECONDS OUT FROM PLAYING PLAY-STATION AND TURNS TO HIS SON)

You alright son?

His son nods his head.

NARRATOR

This happens every week, when he can be bothered to see his son.

 What are we teaching the next generation?

UNFORTUNATLEY, IT'S NOT JUST THE BOYS

Girls just wanna have fun.

Cyndi Lauper.

Parents R Not Us

BABY GIRL

An Original Scenario

By Kevin Treasure

INT. HALLWAY SCENE. DAY

A young female all dressed up in a short black dress makes her way downstairs, trying to finish off her makeup. As she struggles to make her way downstairs a baby girl tries frantically to cling to the legs of her mother.

JANET

Mum, please just put her to bed at 9 o'clock please, she'll go right off to sleep.

MUM

You can't go out again, you're are doing this every weekend

JANET

I want to go out with my friends. (RAISING HER VOICE)

MUM

Your friends haven't got a two-year-old daughter to look after

Baby starts to cry for her mother as she is being passed over to her grandma.

JANET

I won't be late I'll be back about 3 o'clock

MUM

You said that last week. What kind of upbringing are you giving this child if you're never there for her staying out all night? When I was your age I was at home not gallivanting all over the place.

JANET

You're not doing anything now are you? Why is it such a big deal to look after your granddaughter?

MUM

That's not the point; I had to make sacrifices for you when I had you. When my friends were going partying I had to stay home and look after you. You have to give this child a stable home. What kind of example are you setting if you are running out every weekend and sleeping in until one, two o'clock in the afternoon? It's got to stop Janet.

JANET

(*RAISED VOICE*) I'm not going to argue with you mum, are you going to look after her or not?

MUM

(TAKING THE BABY FROM HER DAUGHTER) I'll look after her, but I'm not doing this every weekend.

Baby still crying while mother runs out the door and into a car full of girls.

JANET

(WHILE GETTING IN THE CAR) Make space for me! Come on move up. Hey, Is Tony going to be there tonight? He tried to chat me up the other day; I think he's really cute.

The child's grandma shuts the door while trying to console her granddaughter, who is now screaming for her mother who has now left.

NARRATOR

Going out once or twice is understandable, but every weekend is not wise. Parents are to spend time with their children. Let's re-phrase that. Quality time.

GROUP WORK

You have two options;

1. Using mixed groups of boys and girls each group is to take one of the scenarios and act them out. Feel free to add your own dialogue and actions. After the dramatization of each act in your groups, the main character is to be placed in the hot-seat and is to be questioned individually by the group about the choices they made.

Drama Techniques To Be Used: Forum Theatre, Narration and Marking the moment.

2. Design a 30 second advert for a marketing campaign to highlight the dangers of underage pregnancy?

DISCUSSION TIME

Having a baby is one of the implications of unprotected sex can you think of any others?

In your opinion do you think most young people are aware of the responsibilities that come with parenthood?

Do you know that sex is not the same thing as love? There may be some disagreement, explain ("Sex is physical while love is emotional".)

Would you agree that a certain level of maturity is needed to raise children?

Are most of the friends you know, at that level of maturity?

Do I have cultural, moral or religious convictions that would make it feel wrong for me to have sex? Do you see this as an advantage?

How much do you know about herpes, Aids and other Sexually Transmitted Diseases?

Can you discuss the possibility of pregnancy or STDs with your partner?

Is it possible for you to communicate openly with your partner about things that are really important to you?

How will it affect your relationship if you decide not to have sex?

Babies can decide to cry at any moment of the day or night. Changing nappies can be a very messy and thankless job. Do you think most teenagers can truly handle the disruptions a baby can bring?

At this time in your life would you be a good father/mother?

Do you think the majority of young people are not taught how to be a father/mother?

Are young people aware of the financial burden a child can also bring? They are not cheap.

Young women, who happen to fall into the trap of underage pregnancy, will have to come to terms that their freedom will be jeopardized. Do you think that there is a level of regret that teenage mothers feel that they may be missing out on good times.

List the advantages a baby adds to your life.

Now list the disadvantages.

Which list is longer?

"If you don't hear, you will feel."

Old Caribbean Proverb.

Motherly Love

An Original Screenplay

By Kevin Treasure

A mother and her son sit at a table. The son studies, the mom reads the paper. They're relaxed, enjoying each other's company.

NARRATOR

Here we have an ordinary mother who was forced to raise her son on her own. She always allowed him to attend extracurricular activities, when he was younger she took him to Sunday school and has tried to give him a good upbringing. She has struggled and worked hard. She now has a good home and her son has never been in want. By common standards he is pretty spoilt. She has poured out a lot of money in extra tuition in English and maths and her son has excelled in his class work.

The son gets up from the table and flops himself on the couch. He picks up the TV remote.

NARRATOR

However, as he grows older his mother starts to notice a change in his attitude towards his hobbies

MUM

Aren't you going to football?

DAVID

I stopped going to football.

The son starts flipping channels on the remote control.

MUM

I thought you loved football?

DAVID

I just got bored of it. I don't want to be a footballer.

MUM

What do you want to do then?

DAVID

I don't know. Why you always on my case?

MUM

I'm not on your case. It's just lately you don't seem to care. You're getting up late. I'm getting calls from the school about your behavior and you're coming in later and later every night.

DAVID

(Raised voice) Can't I go out without you treating me like a baby and always questioning me?

MUM

Don't you raise your voice to me? I'm not one of your school friends; you have manners when you're talking to me.

DAVID

(Interrupting) Yeah, Yeah, Whatever mum.

MUM

Get up stairs. How dare you talk to me like that.

Son brushes past his mum as he storms up the stairs murmuring to himself.

NARRATOR

As time goes on her David's behavior goes from bad to worse.

The doorbell rings. Some of the son's friends come over and make their way into the bedroom where they turn on the music and start rolling joints.

NARRATOR

He starts hanging out with the wrong crowd who will eventually get him in trouble. Everyone else can see it except David.

FRIEND 1

Is your mum here?

DAVID

She's downstairs, why?

FRIEND 1

Don't tell anyone. Look what one of the elders gave me to hold.

His friend discretely pulls out a semi automatic weapon and shows it to them.

FRIEND 2

Is it loaded?

FRIEND 1

Of course it's loaded you idiot.

His mother's footsteps are heard coming up the stairs. His friend quickly puts the gun into the waistband of his trousers. His mother opens the door and enters the room.

MUM

What are these boys doing in my house? I don't want these boys in my house.

DAVID

We were just going.

MUM

You're not going anywhere.

She grabs his arm. David jerks his arm away.

MUM

You're not going out with these hoodlums!

DAVID

They're my friends!

MUM

They're troublemakers! I want them out of my house!

DAVID

Fine.

David and his friends put their hoods up and leave the house. Mum runs to the front door.

MUM

Don't go with them!

The youths get into a "car" and drive off. The driver puts the gun underneath the seat next to him.

NARRATOR

His mother's pleas fall upon deaf ears. Her son begins to get into fights and begins a newfound hobby of stealing motorbikes and selling them back on Gumtree. He even goes as far to as to get a tattoo on his neck of his gang affiliation. His life style can only result in one thing. Prison.

As David and his friends drive along the high street they notice a police car behind them, before they can get away the siren goes on and they are pulled over. As the officer approaches the vehicle he notices a scuffle in the back of the car.

OFFICER

Is this your car?

FRIEND 1

It's my friend's car.

OFFICER 2

Your friend's car! Son you look about 16 years old. OK everybody out of the car.

As the officers begin to search the car they find the gun tucked away underneath the seat and £3000 in cash.

OFFICER 1

I suppose this is your friend's to.

DAVID

It's not mine, it's not mine!

FRIEND 1

(Angrily) Shut your mouth. Don't say anything.

NARRATOR

There's an unwritten crime known as guilty by association. The gun did not belong to David, but the police don't know that. As no one takes responsibility for the weapon all the youths are charged and held on remand.

The youths are led into a courtroom. They wait in the dock as the judge makes his summing up. Mum sits in the gallery.

JUDGE

In light of the amount of money found in the vehicle, and the firearms matching that of recent robberies, my minimum sentence for each of the defendants is five years.

The judge bangs the gavel. David looks over at his mum who looks back at him, tearful. She walks away from the courtroom shattered and broken.

NARRATOR

Time and time again he refused to listened to his mother and take sound advice. Now his mum is heartbroken and her son is in prison.

GROUP WORK

Create a scene, which follows on from the last scene of the story.

You can choose to focus on the mother, the son or the son's friends.

It could be the son. His thoughts in his prison cell. He could be experiencing regret, shame or anger. "Why didn't I listen to my mum? The gun wasn't even mine. I don't know anyone in here. I wonder what my girlfriends doing?"

You could focus on his mother's pain. She could be at home or discussing her feelings with a friend. You could focus on the shame she may be feeling, the anguish, anger or disappointment in her son.

It could even be his friends reaction to him in prison. It could be negative or positive. "I knew that David was weak, I should punch him up. He was ready to spill his guts. You wait till we get out."

DISCUSSION TIME

Why does peer pressure make normally good kids do bad things?

Can peer pressure be beaten?

How do you know the difference between *good* peer pressure and *bad* peer pressure?

What are the most common ways that peer pressure shows up?

Peer pressure shows up in a variety of ways, some positive and some negative. On the scale of 1 to 5(one being the highest five being the lowest) discuss and put in order the examples of negative peer pressure:

> Pressure to experiment with drugs or drink alcohol.

> Pressure to vandalise public or private property.

> Pressure to steal.

> Pressure to have a physical confrontation with another teen.

> Pressure to have sex before you're ready.

How can you say no to peer pressure without being made fun of?

If you give in to peer pressure does it mean that you are a follower or that you just have no will of your own?

If your friends were going the wrong way in any given situation would you follow them?

Is it really so bad to be different to stand out from the crowd?

How important is it to listen to your parents?

How important is it to have positive friends?

People have often said if you show me your friends, I will tell you who you are. Are your friends a reflection of who you are?

Why do you think gang culture has grown within our inner cities?

Is there a time in the lives of some young people when they respect the opinions of their friends more than the opinions of their parents?

Do you think that people will judge you according to your company?

Do you think that young people think about the affects their wrong decisions have on their loved ones and the people close to them?

Every parent has high ideals for their children and their concern and guidance is usually their way of trying to protect you from making wrong decisions. Do you think that some young people see this as control?

...and forsaking all others,

keep yourself only unto....

Happily Married

An Original Scenario

By Kevin Treasure

NARRATOR

This guy's got it made. Married with a beautiful wife and two wonderful daughters. A nice home and a very high paid job. By normal standards he is doing exceptionally well. He has managed to increase his company's profits by millions and has just been made an Associate Director.

INT. DAY. OFFICE

Tony and his boss relax back in Tony's new office.

BOSS

Well done, you have managed to turn this company around. This company has never experienced this type of growth and it's all thanks to you. Keep up the good work.

TONY

I'll do my best.

BOSS

You've been dong fine up till now son, oh by the way, Janet's away on annual leave for a few weeks, we have had to hire a temp to cover. She started today, she's a bit of a looker. Careful, you're a married man. (JOKINGLY)

NARRATOR

His boss was right; she is very attractive, and very flirtatious.

The secretary enters Tony's office to bring in his files.

GEORGINA

Is there anything else you need doing?

TONY

No, That will be all for today,

Tony watches her as she leaves his office; she turns and smiles as she leaves.

NARRATOR

The temp has only been with the company two weeks, but Tony has been spending an excessive amount of time with her during and after work.

INT. DAY. HOME

David leaves for work his usual time in his usual manner, his wife sees him off at the door.

WIFE

You have a good day darling; I'll see you when you get back.

HUSBAND

I'll be late home again honey,

WIFE

You were late yesterday,

HUSBAND

I know we got this big contract, which has to be completed this week. I'll make it up to you.

WIFE

You better.

Tony drives off to work.

NARRATOR

These past two weeks, Tony and Georgina have got quite close, a bit too close.

INT. DAY. OFFICE

NARRATOR

Tony and Georgina are locked in a passionate clinch.

GEORGINA

Suppose your wife finds out?

TONY

She won't. (AS HE BEGINS TO PULL HER CLOTHES OFF)

They continue to kiss and embrace.

NARRATOR

This lady is the temp. She's only been there for 3 week's; he's been married for eight years. Some things take a lifetime to build yet moments to destroy. Tony continues his affair for a few months until his wife takes a visit to the health clinic.

Tony has contracted chlamydia and has passed it onto his wife; they have been trying for a boy for sometime chlamydia makes you infertile.

NARRATOR

His wife found out about the affair the hard way. Now his marriage is on the rocks, his wife wants a divorce and his company are in talks about his future, his conduct is not the type of image they wish to portray for their corporation. His life is a mess and he does not know what to do.

Was it worth it?

GROUP WORK

In groups each person is to take on the role of one of the person involved in the above story. You can use the Thought-tracking technique for this group work. This will consist of a person to audience piece, which will consist mainly of improvisation on the actors/actresses part.

Husband: His own thoughts, Regret. How could I let this happen? He could have been thrown out the house, living with his mum, faced with divorce, apologetic, did not know what got into him, he could also be concerned about STD he has contracted.

Wife: Her thoughts and feelings; How could he do this? We had the perfect marriage, he's destroyed everything, we've been together for years, I trusted him, I don't want anything to do with him, he could have given me Aids, I can't have anymore children.

Emotions: Sadness, anger, heartbroken, despair, hopelessness revenge,

Eldest Daughter: Caught between mum and dad, love them both, can't stand the arguing, could be upset at dad, trying to hide it from her baby sister, maybe having trouble at school.

The Secretary: He wanted it, he forced himself on me, I did remind him he was married but he didn't care, he knew what he was getting into. He told me to go to the clinic; I haven't got any STD's.

DISCUSSION TIME

Did Tony really think about his actions? If not, why not?

Do you think he considered the consequences of his affair?

What are the negative effects on the family when people commit adultery?

Do you believe temptation of this type can be avoided, If so how?

Do you think marriage is still held in high regards today?

Do you think it would be more beneficial to teach children the value of marriage and relationships than sex education?

Success, handled wrongly or unprepared can come with its problems, can you name a few?

In what ways can success be the downfall to some people?

Do you believe most young people are properly clued up in regards to STD's?

Wolf in sheeps clothing?

Love Lust

An Original Story

By Kevin Treasure

NARRATOR

Lorraine and her friends have been planning an all girls holiday for months. Destination, Antigua.

INT. BEDROOM. DAYTIME

SONIA

You like? (holding up a yellow bikini to her body)

RIANA

You are not wearing that?

SONIA

Oh, Yes I am. I'm going to Antigua. (doing a little dance)

Turning to Lorraine.

SONIA

What are you bringing?

LORRAINE

Nothing as extravagant as what you're wearing. I'm going for a holiday, not to be harassed by the locals.

SONIA

Yeah, Right Ms Lonely hearts, you and I know why you're going to Antigua. (Raising her eyebrows quickly up and down while smiling)

Lorraine throws the pillow at her.

The girls make their way to the airport, and in 8 hours they're in Antigua.

EXT. BEACH. DAY

RIANA

This is what I'm talking about. Sun, Sea, Men.

LORRAINE

I'm going to the bar, who wants a drink?

It's free. All inclusive means drink till you drop.

Riana nods.

SONIA

Don't ask dumb questions. Get cigarettes as well.

LORRAINE

Those aren't free

Lorraine walks off towards the bar restaurant area and stops at the bar and rings the bell.

LORRAINE

Service, service please (ringing the bell)

A dark muscular male emerges from the back of the bar carrying a case of drinks.

ALEX

Sorry, How can I help you?

Lorraine smiles

LORRAINE

Two rum and cokes and a Bacardi Breezer please.

ALEX

Where you from London, England?

I've always wanted to visit London.

I heard they have the nicest women with the most beautiful smiles. (Staring into Lorraine's eyes)

Lorraine gives a girlie giggle.

NARRATOR

Boy meets Girl. Boy likes Girl. Girl likes Boy. Girl spends rest of Holiday with Boy.

For the next few days Alex and Lorraine spend the rest of the holiday together, playing beach volleyball, on the Jet Ski's, scuba diving and other recreational activities.

While Sonia and Riana are sidelined.

INT. HOTEL ROOM. DAY

RIANA

Are you going to spend the rest of the holiday with this guy?

SONIA

This was meant to be a girls holiday Lorraine.

LORRAINE

I really like him, he's really fun, he hasn't got any kids, and I think this is the one. No, really I mean it. He's different. He's not seeing anyone.

SONIA

Don't you mean he's not seeing anyone (pause) this week?

Lorraine rolls her eyes.

LORRAINE

No, seriously, He is different; I've never felt like this about anyone before. I think I'm falling in love with him.

Riana looks at Lorraine in despair.

RIANA

HELLO, HELLO, Lorraine. It's a holiday remember. Don't get all romantic on us. You're having fun, he's having fun. That's all it is.

SONIA

And he's not the best looking guy on the block.

LORRAINE (sympathetically)

This isn't jealousy is it, my sisters. (In a wining voice)

RIANA

Get a life.

SONIA

Pleaseeeeeee, I don't want you getting deep on us. I just want to have a good time. We've got four days left. What should we do tonight?

LORRAINE

Alex is taking me to a club.

Sonia and Riana look at each other.

LORRAINE

You two are coming too, and he said something about bringing some friends. (Raising her eyebrows)

Lorraine walks over to them and hugs them as they all burst into smiles.

LORRAINE

Would I let my girls down?

RIANA

They better be good looking?

SONIA

Better looking than your man?

LORRAINE

I hope not. (walking out the room laughing)

EXT. BAR. NIGHT

Riana and Sonia are seated next to two fat local guys looking very disappointed. Sonia folds her arms and pulls her skirt down. While Riana tries her best to edge away from her overweight companion. While Lorraine and Alex are in tight clinch on the dance floor.

RIANA

I've had enough of this crap; I'm going back to my room.

SONIA

Can you excuse me please?

Sonia and Riana both get up and leave their table, leaving their companions sipping on pepsi.

RIANA

Lorraine, are you coming?

Lorraine shakes her head.

LORRAINE

I'll meet you back at the hotel.

RIANA

Lorraine we came together

LORRAINE

I'll be O.K.

RIANA

(WHISPERING) I got a bad feeling about this you don't even know him.

LORRAINE

I'm not stupid, I aint going to do nothing

RIANA

I just don't trust him, Just come back to the hotel.

LORRAINE

You're such a killjoy; I'll be back later.

As the music plays, Lorraine and Alex continue to slow dance. Slow music plays in the background.

INT. HOTEL ROOM.NIGHT

Alex and Sonia lay on the couch as Alex tries to force himself upon Lorraine.

LORRAINE

No, I just want to be with you. Stop.

Alex continues to press upon Lorraine and becomes more forceful.

LORRAINE

You're hurting me get off. Stop please stop.

Alex now restraining Lorraine, tears off her top and tries to undo her skirt. A loud banging at the door interrupts him.

LORRAINE

Get off me.

Lorraine pushes him off and runs to the door. She opens it to find Riana and Sonia, desperately trying to get in.

SONIA

What's going on?

LORRAINE

(Almost in tears) He tried to rape me.

ALEX

Shut up you liar. You wanted it. (Aggressively)

LORRAINE

You liar. Call the police.

RIANA

Call the police Sonia.

ALEX

Call the police, who they going to believe you or me? First thing they're going to ask is what you doing in my room at 03:00 in the morning. Call them; you can use my phone if you like (sarcastically.)

LORRAINE

(Looking to Sonia and Riana) Let's just go.

SONIA

You can't just leave it like that.

LORRAINE

I just want to go home.

Lorraine walks out. Sonia and Riana walk out after her.

RIANA

You can't just leave it like this. Don't let him get away with this.

SONIA

I knew he was a rat. I never trusted him from the start.

They make their way back to their hotel room.

RIANA

Lorraine, I know you're shaken up right now, but we got to call the police. He can't treat you like that. He tried to rape you and he's acting like nothing's wrong.

LORRAINE

It means police and questioning and it will just be my word against his. I don't want to go through all that, besides nothing happened. I just want to go home.

Lorraine walks off leaving Sonia and Riana bewildered.

GROUP WORK

In groups of 4-5 sit down and plan a courtroom scene in regards to the story you have just read. The case could be biased towards Lorraine or Alex. You can only use the information you have read in the play for the case. This may need to be scripted, and may run over a few sessions.

Characters you will need are as follows:

Lorraine

Alex

Riana

Sonia

Judge

Prosecution

Defence

DISCUSSION TIME

Do you feel that most young women are made aware of the dangers of date rape?

What attitudes and practices make date rape more likely to occur in some settings?

Example: Social settings, parties, clubs, holidays, etc.

What type of attitudes and practices exhibited in men are warning signs for women to avoid? E.g.: anger, forceful personality, etc.

Do you believe people are more unwilling to report crime when the suspects are known?

Why don't rape and attempted rape victims report crime to the police?

Do you believe the stress and pressure of courtrooms can usually deter people from pressing charges in regards to crime?

Do you believe that alcohol and drugs play a large role in rape and attempted rape cases?

Do you believe there are factors that make people more vulnerable to rape? (E.g.: drugs, drink, and isolation.)

Do you believed some men misinterpret body language, casual talk, or gestures, as sexual come-ons?

What do you believe can be done to prevent men who try to take advantage of women in this way?

What do you do when you see your friends involved in a relationship, which you perceive to be unhealthy or dangerous?